A PUMA POINT PRODUCTION LLC
SUBSIDIARY OF

ARTIST LLC

One day Colt saw a tiny horse fall out of a big horse.

The big horse licked and cleaned the little horse.

At first the little horse could barely stand.

The next day the little colt was running all over the field

God made all life; boys and girls, colts and fillies

There are mountain lions in the country where Colt lives.

One day the little pony was all alone.

Colt loved him and tamed him but the colt was a wild one.

Colt realized his pony had private parts like his own.

"I remember when I was ten and fell in love with my teacher. Thinking back it was silly but we sometimes have silly feelings that we don't understand".

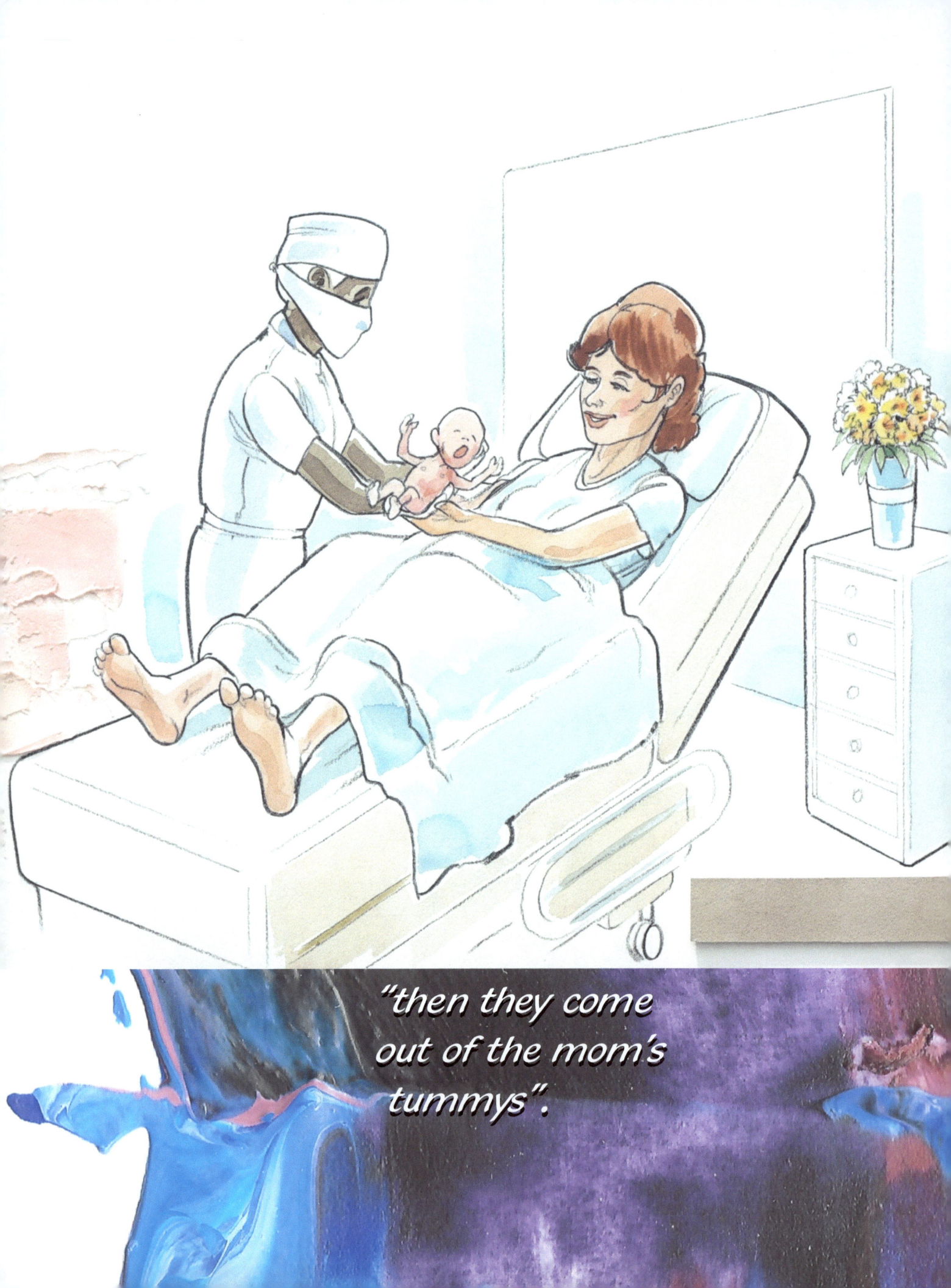

"then they come out of the mom's tummys".

That's how God makes families, horses, birds, flowers, trees, bees, and all living things.

Colt grew taller and stronger over the passing years and his pony grew into a big and powerful stallion.

Dad had a filly. The colt and the filly liked each other but Dad kept them in separate meadows.

One day Colt and Lilly married and they lived happily because they knew Jesus as their Savior and friend and they had been taught God's rules for marriage.

# Colt's Wild Stallion
### AN ICE BREAKER BOOK

Most men think about it all the time but "nobody talks about it" at least not in a healthy helpful manner. Women think about it. Boys and girls think about it. People can joke about it but most cannot have a mature conversation about it. It is usually swiftly swept under the rug in polite company. It's sex. We are living in a time when God's great gift of procreation is subverted and perverted in almost every area of life. Television, movies, news media, even our homes, churches are invaded by perversion. Great religious organizations struggle with corruption within their ranks due to the deadly silence. Companies large and small have been ruined by the exposure of sexual corruption within. Great men and women have fallen when their moral failure becomes public. Families, one after another, are damaged and ruined due to sexual abuse. Most movies have as a main theme; adultery of one kind or another. It seems that those who entertain and thereby also educate our culture cannot tell a story without moral failure as the basis of the script. Divorce, remarriage, mistresses, sleeping together without the courageous commitment of marriage, sodomy are pushed by the media as norms. The culture of much of the United States of American and the world at large seems to be in a steep moral pitfall. The results are tragic. We ALL struggle with the sex drive and it's issues.

I'm optimistic that those who will can help their children escape the corruption and deal with their own desires constructively. Thus this book. You can use this book as one of your tools to prepare your child in a fun and positive way for the inevitable. If your child is not properly educated by you by age eight their little and older friends will definitely corrupt them with great damage and erroneous information and they will corrupt each other. Children are curious and need your help. I encourage you to also get other books in this vein that will help you with other areas of sexuality; a book or two as time goes along with specific sex education. This book is designed to only "break the ice". You can use the metaphors built into the design, such as; the stallion is born black but turns white as it grows, also it becomes very strong and much larger as it matures, etc. This book is not designed as the answer to all the questions. Forewarned is forearmed. I encourage you to candidly go over Bible portions like Genesis chapters 1 and 2, Leviticus chapter 18, Deuteronomy 22, etc. God created sex. All life multiplies through that process. God made it to be fun. The Devil did not make sex, but he seems to have taken over the territory. If we don't take the initiative the corruption around us will and the results will be tragic.

When I was five I witnessed a grown man molest a six month old baby. I didn't understand what I was seeing. He said, "it was good for her". Sadly the people closest to us are potentially the ones most likely to molest. Family members, friends, even friends in church, the work place, etc. are not exempt from the potential of molestation. I knew a man who not only was having sex with his wife, but also his daughter and his grand daughter. He was a respected church member. Another man I knew was a youth leader. He had a hidden reputation for repeated and continuous adultery. He had his "hooks" into the pastor and thus was "forgiven" his continuos offenses. Pedophiles patrol even our churches, hidden as friends; even church workers sometimes. You, no doubt can supply your own stories. Sadly we MUST always be on the alert to educate and protect our children. This book can aid you immensely in doing just that. God considers the issue so important that He demanded the death penalty for many of the acts that the world at large just ignores by silence. What most people embarrassingly quickly "sweep under the rug" God told Moses to read aloud in public. Death was even demanded for most perversion. How far afield the world has gone! For getting a girl pregnant out of wedlock the penalty was death (Deuteronomy chapter 22). Just to say "don't" will not protect your youngster. Obviously the Creator who gave us this powerful gift takes its' abuse much more seriously than we do. I believe that we are losing the United States of America and the world at large over this issue. Isaiah 57:5; The nation of Israel was forced out of their ancient land over the issues of pornography and abortion and we are not exempt from that judgement. .

You can find this book useful as a bridge to the young mind of your child to accomplish the most important task of helping them gain a healthy outlook on sex. You can use it as a "springboard" to related issues, healthy conversations, and guidance for their good and the glory of God. God bless you on the exciting path of life and your endeavors towards mental, spiritual, and sexual health. BREAK THE ICE, START THE CONVERSATION EARLY!

Ed French

www.ingramcontent.com/pod-product-compliance
Lightning Source LLC
Chambersburg PA
CBHW041232040426

42444CB00002B/135